This past summer,  storm was coming up. I saw something bobbing in the waves close to the shore. I paddled over and found a sealed, welded metal box. Curious, I picked it up. I put it aside when I got home and got busy and didn't think about it for several days. One Saturday afternoon, I put it in a vice and took a hacksaw to it. After about ten minutes, I had it open and was very surprised at what was inside. I found a handwritten journal and a golden locket in a dilapidated leather pouch. Engraved on the locket were the words, "God bless you, Molly darling, my straying soul you saved." The date "June 13, 1925" was also engraved. The journal contained a poem which had been elegantly handwritten with a fountain pen. Some of the pages were waterlogged and nearly unreadable. It took me several weeks to decipher the writing.

I had the locket and the box analyzed. The locket was said to be 18 carat gold and at least ninety years old. I was told that the box had probably been floating in the water for at least ten years. The box had many scrapes and dents, as if it had been battered by the rocks on a journey down the Chattooga River. Other than the names in the poem, I found nothing to indicate who wrote the poem or why it and the locket were placed in the box. The poem was reconstructed to the best of my ability. The poem follows.

Joel Coke

The Ghost of Woodall Shoals

or

The Demon's Deliverance

The Ghost of Woodall Shoals

THE GHOST OF WOODALL SHOALS
OR
THE DEMON'S DELIVERANCE

Legend is often much revered, and the truth can be maligned;
Regrettably, at the loss of truth, they can both be intertwined.
I have a Chattooga River story where legend and truth contend,
But until I've given all the facts, my position I'll suspend.

On our search for answers, down the river we will ride
And journey over waters where legend and truth collide.
There's a place up in the foothills where the western border lies,
Where the Chattooga flips and tumbles and the wild whitewater flies.

The place is Woodall Shoals, where the rapids tell the story,
A mystic range of river where danger swirls in glory
Where the waters come together in a rocky, wild conflation
And the river there at Woodall pours an infamous oblation.

It's a place arrayed with rapids and wicked, swirling holes,
Where there's a legend in the water called the Ghost of Woodall Shoals,
A place to stay away from, or so the locals tell —
They say the shoals are haunted by a fiend straight out of hell.

The story goes way back to the time of prohibition,
When hops and malts and barley made a useful coalition.
There lived an evil moonshiner named Willard McVeigh
Who was a bootlegging man who had his own way.

He was big and cagey and known for his wrath
And people walked easy when they walked on Willard's path.
It was said that he'd robbed, beaten, and killed —
It was a hard field of sin that Willard had tilled.

But Willard loved a woman by the name of Molly Cole
Who could touch the only soft spot on old Willard's soul.
She was a striking-looking woman with raven hair,
With steel-blue eyes and a countenance fair.

Willard was stricken with his very first sight
Of this beautiful woman on a soft summer night.
Though an outlaw man who was dangerous and wild,
Willard fell for Molly like a lovestruck child.

By the woman's love he was totally taken,
And his hell-raising ways were suddenly shaken.
When Molly heard of Willard's past, she found it all alarming,
But when he smiled and took her hand, he was absolutely charming.

She was troubled and endangered, but reckless and bold,
And it was to the rakish Willard that her hasty heart was sold.
It was with a righteous resignation to his sinful past
That Molly married Willard, and her love was cast.

It was quite a feather in Molly's cap when Willard quit his drinking,
But when Willard tithed and went to church, people started thinking
That under Molly's guidance it amazingly seemed
She'd change old Willard more than anyone dreamed.

He got a job at a sawmill turning logs into lumber
With a circular saw making planks by the number.
Willard was different and pleased beyond measure
And was totally happy with Molly as his treasure.

He gave his love a golden locket with the precious words engraved,
"God bless you, Molly darling, my straying soul you saved."
With the locket clasped at Molly's neck and Willard's life redeemed,
Into their lives for several years love and bounty streamed.

But with timber prices falling fast in a time of great depression,
Willard lost his sawmill job and others in quick succession.
Things broke down and the times got worse,
And Willard was blighted with a terrible curse.

Willard was weak and it wasn't too long
Before he started going bad and things went wrong.
Molly got the feeling he was running around,
And with a younger woman he was finally found.

Willard was a victim of his wicked obsessions
But his love for Molly transcended transgressions.
He spurned the younger woman and left her alone,
And he went back to Molly and tried to atone.

Molly held the hatred of a woman deceived
And in her vengeful heart retribution conceived.
She was a hot-blooded woman, and her hot blood showed
And Willard got a glimpse of the devil she rode.

Molly threw the golden locket in Willard's face,
Then she cussed old Willard all over the place.
Molly fought with Willard and she pulled out a knife —
She made a thrust at Willard, nearly ending his life.

She took the knife and waved it around and made a wicked slash,
She cut his hand and stabbed his arm and left a vicious gash.
He grabbed her wrist with a bloody hand and gripped her very tightly;
Molly struggled and dropped the knife, but her eyes flashed very brightly.

Willard McVeigh was a dangerous man and his ways were much deplored,
But his eyes were calm and he posed no threat, for his Molly he adored.
He draped the locket over Molly's dress and spoke of their love's inception
And tried to make amends to her for his wicked and evil deception.

Willard held his precious Molly close in a favored firm embrace
And sweetly stroked her wonderful hair and kissed her pretty face.
He spoke of their love and their natural attraction;
"You go and be damned," was her natural reaction.

Willard backed away and looked his woman in the eye;
He wept when he did it, but he told her goodbye.
There were tears in Molly's eyes when her man walked away,
And she stroked the bloody locket where the locket lay.

Into Willard's breaking heart something sinister crept,
All along the river where he wandered and wept.
On the ragged edge of sadness, Willard fell to desperation
And searched and found the bottle as his only inspiration.

The man got meaner and was worse than before,
Since he couldn't talk to Molly or see her anymore.
In dreary contemplation of Molly's rejection,
Broken-hearted Willard made an evil selection.

He moved to the woods and started making shine
By the river in a shack surrounded by pine.
On a stormy evening he was tending his trade
When the tax men found him on a liquor-still raid.

There were several men around his shack and Willard was surrounded;
He knew he'd have to run or fight or he would be impounded.
He took his rifle and fired a shot to keep them at a distance
To let them know that he would fight and give them fierce resistance.

A bullet flew through Willard's still and pierced the copper kettle.
The fight was on, and they shot again and aroused old Willard's mettle.
He aimed his gun and fired away, and his manhood he asserted:
He cleared a path with a shotgun blast and left his shack deserted.

Amidst hoots and yells and barking dogs and stormy twilight thunder,
It was no time to cower down or make a foolish blunder.
In the wind and rain he heard the sound of rifle fire that crackled;
If he were caught, he'd go to jail and on the chain gang shackled.

Through the drenching rain he ran in a wild, erratic scramble —
He ripped his clothes and tore his face on the briar, the brush, and the bramble.
He made it through the stormy woods to the splashing riverside,
Where underneath the waving trees his waiting boat was tied.

Big Willard had to make his way in the ebbing of twilight
Or take a chance and run the rapids in the darkness of the night.
Willard rode the rising stream with his chances growing dire
As lightning skewered the darkened clouds and splattered them with fire.

With the thrashing waters mixing in a big, white water tangle,
Willard took his wooden boat through the crashing river wrangle.
When at first the river broke across his open bow,
He paddled hard and moved ahead, and the rapids he did plow.

Though Willard knew the river well, he was still concerned,
And when he ran at Woodall Shoals his boat was overturned.
He tumbled in the rapids and flailed beneath his craft,
Then made it to the surface and grabbed his paddle's shaft.

He called out Molly's name as he yelled one last lament
And asked her for forgiveness before his life was finally spent.
As lightning struck at Woodall Shoals and evening turned to night,
The river overwhelmed him and dragged him out of sight.

Though no trace was ever seen and his body never found,
It was said and widely believed that Willard McVeigh had drowned.
Molly wandered by the river near the rocks where Willard fled
In the waning, forlorn hope that Willard wasn't dead.

As Molly walked, she wore the locket, and from her neck it swayed,
And as she walked she tried her best to have the truth delayed.
After searching for an anxious week and a couple of anxious days,
Molly went back to her lonely home and kept solitary ways.

When Molly lost her wayward Willard, she was broken and harshly branded,
Burdened by the constant grief that her clawing conscience commanded.
For the rest of her long and tragic life, Molly was never to marry
And it was the memory of Willard's death that Molly would always carry.

The river flowed and so did time, and stories and legends began,
All about a twilight ghost where the Woodall rapids ran.
Years had washed against the shoals since Willard made his run,
Yet when a storm was falling down and the day was nearly done,

It was said the cold Chattooga still flowed over Willard's bones,
And if you listened closely you could hear old Willard's moans
At that place called Woodall where the Chattooga rolled and worked
They said on stormy twilights a red-eyed demon lurked.

There was a tale among the locals that some took just on faith,
A ghastly horror story of a murdering river wraith.
"Best not go down by Woodall," was how the story went
Where the river took a turn and the water was in descent.

Whether by rapids or by ghost, they were done;
The deaths there at Woodall numbered thirty and one.
Most blamed the rapids, but some would say
It was the murdering ghost of old Willard McVeigh.

Decades later, a chapter was written that enhances our story's pages
And added to the river lore in some of its various stages.
The story took a mysterious turn when a woman was selected
To bring about a destiny that no one ever suspected.

She was tired of the books and the college providers
And came to spend the summer with the whitewater riders.
Her name was Leah and she came for the season —
A sense of adventure was a viable reason.

She was a strong-willed woman in the prime of her youth
And was searching for excitement and advancing the truth.
Through the forest like a ribbon of blue and white and green
The Chattooga lay before her like nothing she'd ever seen.

The river could be hard, and it could be very tragic,
But Leah's mind was taken with its whitewater magic.
Among river bums and river nymphs and wild whitewater sages,
She sought to learn the river's ways as she watched the river's rages.

She met a boater named Bobby, and by the river they walked,
All about the summer and the rapids they talked.
He was tall and blond and his body was tight,
And he could skim a set of rapids like a bird in flight.

He was flashy and bold with an arrogant flare —
Bobby wouldn't back off, and he'd take any dare.
He was a blue-eyed rogue and his days consisted
Of the blandishments from women that he never resisted.

Leah didn't like it, and she could always bet
That he had a flirtation with every woman he met.
She always forgave him and forgave his deceit,
For he was real good-looking and his kisses were sweet.

He took Leah in hand, and he knew what to do
To show her the river and a good time, too.
He put her in a kayak where he gave her revelation
Baptizing her with river spray that gave her dedication.

What Bobby didn't teach her, Leah learned all alone;
She found the river's freedom and she made it her own.
On the river she was breathless and seized by fascination
As the rapids made her spirits soar beyond exhilaration.

She wore tie-dyed shirts and cut-off blue jeans
Like a hard-driving, river-running woman of means.
As Bobby watched her ride against the whitewater splendor,
His appreciation rose and his affection grew tender.

She was a long-haired beauty in the summer befalling;
Bobby fell in love, and he found her enthralling.
He gave his wandering heart to her despite its past distractions
And concentrated all his love on Leah's many attractions.

Their love was abundant and without any ration;
It was grounded in joy, and it was bonded by passion.
They rode the numinous river beneath the sky, between the trees
And all their moments of happiness they found and tried to seize.

All summer the river flowed like blood through the veins of earth,

Revealing to them a timelessness of the Chattooga's wonderful worth.

The summer rolled by, and Bobby sought without a single doubt

To seek the river legend that he'd always heard about.

"Best not go down by Woodall" was all he'd ever heard

But foolish talk of red-eyed ghosts, Bobby thought absurd.

He ridiculed the tales as superstitious lore,

All hoary fabrications of childish, grisly gore.

He was stoked for the rapids and was ready and keen

To head out in the twilight where the ghost was seen.

On a rock by the river in the evening he stood,

Plotting out the river where the running was good.

Leah came up and she took him by the hand,

And they both left the rock and walked through the sand.

Down the river with her Bobby she knew that she should go,

But he smiled into her pretty eyes, and then he told her no.

She was worried for his safety and she wanted to ride
Down the river with her Bobby and be by his side.
He kissed her on the mouth and he kissed her on the cheek
And went to run the rapids with the river at peak.

She loved her Bobby dearly and she watched from the shore
As he moved through the rapids and the river's roar.
As clouds rolled in and hung down low with falling evening rain,
Leah stood and watched him go and waved to him in vain.

The sky threw down its forked fire with sounds like slamming walls;
Leah ran and yelled to him, but he never heard her calls.
Why Bobby wouldn't let her go, she never could discern;
She watched him paddle out of sight and awaited his return.

They found his body lifeless and swirling in the holes,
A victim of the rapids or the Ghost of Woodall Shoals.
Her Bobby ran at Woodall, and her Bobby wound up dead.
"Best not go down by Woodall" was what the locals said.

"Best not go down by Woodall," the people told her, too;
To not go down by Woodall was what she couldn't do.
What happened to her Bobby she really had to know,
So through those swirling rapids she really had to go.

She was guilt-ridden and troubled and terribly depressed,
It was over Bobby's death that she constantly obsessed.
Leah sought some elder wisdom from a legendary lady –
She found her near the river where the woods were dark and shady.

Down a red clay road on a path through the trees,
She sat on Molly's porch and caught a cooling breeze.
Molly now had long gray hair and was withered and very old
But with flashing fire in her vivid eyes and a mighty spirit untold.

Molly was frail and visibly weak and her hands did vaguely tremble,
As memories of her ancient past she recalled and tried to assemble.
She spoke about Willard and the love that he'd needed
And of all of her pleadings that had gone unheeded.

It was her affection for Willard that she widely displayed
But it was old Willard's ways that left her quite dismayed.
With her hand on Leah's shoulder, she looked at her sadly.
"You know we've both been hurt and hurt really badly;

There's a common kind of weakness that to women is fatal.
It's born in the womb, and it's sealed in the cradle
With a certain kind of man, what's a woman to do?
They give you outlaw-loving and they lie to you, too.

You have a deep obsession and it's driving you mad,
It's causing you more trouble than you've ever had.
If you go down to Woodall, there's hell to pay –
A demon roams the rapids, and it's Willard McVeigh.

Lots of people tried it, and they all went down;
If you go out to Woodall, you will probably drown."
Leah was receptive and was thoughtful and kind,
But she looked at Molly softly and then she spoke her mind.

Leah said that she was going and through hell she would ride
To find the truth of Woodall where her Bobby had died.
Leah was respectful while she watched Molly frown,
But she was going out to Woodall and was not backing down.

Molly looked at Leah closely with a growing resignation
And knew there was no way to stop her dangerous inclination.
"I don't condone what you're doing, but I'm sure that you can
With your obsessive obligation after losing your man.

I've been through the fire of love's desolation;
It's hard to live your life with no consolation.
We lost our men at Woodall, and that gives us a bond.
You're a fine young woman, and of you I am fond."

In front of Molly's blouse there was a locket that dangled;
It was heavy with chain, and it was beautifully spangled.
"The night that Willard walked away, this locket he did clasp –
Around my neck he placed the chain with a sure and certain grasp.

I cut him twice and made him bleed, but Willard didn't care –
Around my neck he hung this locket, and with love he placed it there.
Around my neck it's hung there since, and it's never been removed.
To this locket and to Willard's love I've always been behooved.

A fool I was to let him go while adhering to my pride,
I watched him leave and acted wrong in ways I can't abide."
It was a golden locket on a golden chain
Which Molly unfastened with emotional pain.

Molly took off the locket and the pain she ignored
And it was with these words that Leah was implored:
"Willard gave me this locket as a token of affection
I want you to wear it for your own protection.

Wear this locket when on the water you ramble
To keep you safe from harm on your Woodall gamble."
Leah took away the locket and left Molly alone
And headed for the river and a truth unknown.

She went and got her kayak and determined she was ready
And took it to the shore and slid it in an eddy.
Leah had no fear of Woodall or the danger in wait;
She floated in the current and prepared for her fate.

She paddled down the river as the day began to fade
And listened to the rushing that the swirling water made.
It was in the clouded sky that a storm began to roar —
The thunder broke out loudly and the rain began to pour.

She rode the surging waves as her kayak was slapped
And dodged the broken rocks on which the river lapped.
The light of day was waning fast with darkness on the rise;
She paddled hard and moved ahead and heard the rapid's cries.

Lightning streaked from a cloudy cleft and struck a standing stone,
But Leah bobbed in a rapid's swell and rode the storm alone.
Up ahead was Woodall, and there she would know why
At the place called Woodall her Bobby had to die.

With her wet hair swinging in the raging wind
And the rain and the rapids in a stormy blend
She approached the rocky turn, where the current was stronger.
To find the truth of Woodall, she waited no longer.

There was a low-pitched moan that caught her attention —
She looked through the rain to the point of contention.
There was something in the grayness near the water on a rock
That sent her heart to pounding and her mind near into shock.

Against a sky made ragged by the lightning flash
Through the cold rain driven by the west wind's lash
Before her in the twilight in the midst of the storm
Stood the hulking apparition of a spectral form.

In old dungarees and worn-out boots and a ripped-up shirt he stalked
And the wind blew through his bedraggled hair as in the storm he walked.
While Leah fought the wind and rain and ran the river mazes
The specter howled before her there with eyes like crystal blazes.

It was a towering visitation from the realm of lost, dead souls
That strode upon the river rock as the Ghost of Woodall Shoals.
She saw it stand within the storm and watched it weave and sway
And knew it was the dangerous ghost of the evil Willard McVeigh.

The rapids splashed, the demon raged, and Leah watched with awe
And through the storm with perfect poise her paddle she did draw.
The demon leaped from rock to rock and waited on the shoals
It turned its head and looked at her with eyes like glowing coals.

The demon howled throughout the rain and screamed above the thunder;
Leah steadied and held her own and watched in fearsome wonder.
With lightning falling all around and daylight growing dim,
The demon danced upon the rock and bade her come to him.

She reached into her rain-soaked shirt and found it in her pocket
And pulled the chain around her neck that was holding Molly's locket.
While the red-eyed wraith with its menacing stare
Held her in its gaze through its tangled hair,

Leah manned her sturdy craft with skilled, heroic calm
And waited for the soothing truth to ladle out its balm.
It was near the rock in the river where the demon wailed
That she took the demon's measure as he shouted and railed.

Through the rain and toward the demon on the water she did brave
As she moved beside a frothing, whitened, amorphous, standing wave.
The apparition leaped from the rock and on her kayak fell
And it kneeled upon the craft and rode the rapids well.

When Leah saw Willard's awful eyes and the scars that Molly placed,
She understood the dreadful horror with which she now was faced.
Though most would be afraid to death and all would be confounded,
With Bobby's love her thoughts were clear and her courage seemed unbounded.

Though Willard knelt upon her boat, through the water she did paddle;
Prepared with hope, she had no fear of the evil she would battle.
The demon waved a fiery hand from wall to river wall
And slowed the coming pace of time and slowed the river's fall.

With frozen light upon the sight of a storm that hung in space,
Time was stopped and the river stilled, with raindrops held in place.
Leah looked upon the twilit world and found she was amazed
At all the still and silent things on which her eyes now gazed.

A frozen splash against a rock had mesmerized her mind
And Leah found that she was caught within the demon's bind.
Like a perfect printed image on a vintage postal card,
She saw a lurid lightning bolt by which the sky was scarred.

Like ragged snow the rapids lay against the rigid stolen time,
And once again Leah turned to face the demon in his prime.
Nothing moved but he and she as he perched upon her boat —
The river was stilled as solid glass, and upon it they did float.

Leah looked in Willard's vengeful face and made an evaluation
And spoke in stern and steadfast ways and gave her declaration:
"I've searched the river for the truth, and now the truth I've found —
It's you that took my love from me, and it's here where he was drowned.

I've come this way for recompense, and recompense I'll find
As I ride the falling river and watch the truth unwind."
The demon spoke in an evil voice with a sound like river gravel
And tried to break her courage down and make it all unravel.

Big Willard said, "I've got you now, and you'll die here in the shoals.
Your life will end, and you'll never live to complete your earthly goals.
As for your love, I took your love and made of him a tether
To pull your soul in a river hole, where you'll swirl in hell together.

You're a gutsy girl, but while you swirl, you'll make this demon bolder,
To bring more souls to Woodall Shoals and make their bodies colder."
Leah heard the demon's rant, and though she was in danger,
She straightened up and looked ahead and faced the evil stranger.

Leah smiled a knowing smile, for she had not desponded,
And to the threats that Willard posed, Leah then responded:
"I didn't come to run and hide or grovel away in fear,
So listen while I speak to you, and I'll make my statements clear.

The risks I take and the pain I feel compose a feeble token
To pay the price for Bobby's love that will always go unbroken.
The time has come to state my case and seek some resolution
And rid the river of your kind in a Woodall Shoals ablution.

It's not full compensation but I'll celebrate the loss
When your bones are washed away as random river dross."
She screamed into the demon's face with its eyes of molten flame:
"Willard McVeigh, you killed my man, and I curse your wretched name!"

Big Willard laughed at Leah's curse as if to tempt her ire
And raised his arm above his head with a hand of flaming fire.
"Your life is done and you are through, and I'll take your soul to sunder,
And you'll remain for all of time this river demon's plunder."

The demon clapped its fiery hands, and the river came to life —
Lightning dazzled and thunder rumbled, with time now running rife.
The raindrops fell, the wind blew hard, and the current was still strong,
While the rapids frothed and the demon rode as the kayak moved along.

Old Willard grabbed Leah's long brown hair and quickly dragged her down
Into the river's cold, wet depths, where she would surely drown.
As thoughts of death filled Leah's head, she was scared beyond conception,
And all she got when she struggled on was a cold and wet reception.

There was no way for Leah to swim and there was no way to stand;
She was held by the surging river and by the evil demon's hand.
Over grinding gravel and broken stones her body was dragged and grated;
It seemed to her that she would die as Willard McVeigh had stated.

There was a grip around her pretty throat like she was being strangled;
She raised her hand to break the grasp with the golden chain entangled.
When Willard grabbed the locket chain that held Molly's dear remembrance,
There was made in the angry storm a cry of sweet deliverance.

The cry was heard in last twilight so sublime it seemed to capture
And reveal an essence of some ancient primal rapture.
The twilight winked and disappeared but somehow seemed to savor
One last appeal for one last hope for one last demonic favor.

Somewhere in the darkness wet the grip was then released,
And to the surface Leah swam, and her agony suddenly ceased.
She struggled to the rocky shore, where she faltered and nearly fainted,
With the remnants of her waning strength all tattered, torn, and tainted.

With twilight gone she stumbled on, and her stumbles were repeated;
It was there at the shoals that Leah collapsed like a wet rag doll depleted.
The winds grew calm, thunder stopped, and the clouds were soon dispersed —
With a silver moon and silver stars, the night was reimbursed.

The sky was wide, the air was clear, and the river was pristine;
Though Leah slept on a rocky bed, her sleep was quite serene.
The stars grew dim and hard to see and finally faded away,
And Leah awoke from a needed sleep to the light of another day.

Her shirt was torn, her skin was scraped, and her neck was stiff and sore;
She remembered what had happened to her and was shaken to the core.
Leah's mind was churning wondrous fast in the midst of great confusion.
Was what she'd seen and heard last night real or just delusion?

She searched the shores of Woodall Shoals and found the validation
Of everything that had happened to her, and she smiled with jubilation.
As Leah looked, she saw the truth in the glow of early morning:
A skeletal hand lay on the shore with a golden chain adorning.

The bones were by the shining water, lying in the sand,
With the golden locket tightly held in Willard's honey hand.
Leah took away the spangled locket and buried the whitened bones
And left a sandy, unmarked grave surrounded with river stones.

Leah walked from there to Molly's house though it was miles away
To take and tell the truth to her before the end of day.
She told the tale to Molly, and her heart was there enraptured
As she marveled at the love within the locket there encaptured.

Tears fell on the locket when to Molly it was handed,
Holding memories of the past in which Molly's heart was stranded.
As the locket dangled and the chain she caressed,
Molly thought of her life and the past she accessed.

"Willard was wrong, but I was too, and I drove him to destruction,
But I'll think no more of evil things or grief of my own construction.
My life's been hard and full of pain, but now the past is finished;
I know it's happened late to me, but my soul is now replenished."

Molly turned to Leah, and she looked at her hard —
"There ain't no use in playing life's misery card.
Listen to me, Leah, I've got something to say:
Your obligation's over and you've nothing to pay.

Put your past behind you and let go of your strife;
There ain't no room for trouble in a young girl's life."
As Leah listened to Molly, she took it all to heart
And thought about the new life that she would like to start.

Leah made a special gesture to the lady with silver hair
To thank her for her tenderness and feelings she'd tried to share.
She took the locket from Molly's hands and placed it around her neck,
And as she clasped the golden chain she kept no tears in check.

She embraced the older woman and looked into her wrinkled face.
"I want to be a woman like you with strength and style and grace.
You're a fine woman, Molly, and of you I am fond;
We lost our men at Woodall, and that gives us a bond.

Thank you for your help and for the locket that you loaned,
It freed me from the demon and the grief that had me owned."
In front of Molly's blouse there was a locket that dangled,
It was heavy with chain and it was beautifully spangled.

"The night that Willard walked away, your locket he did clasp
Around your neck he placed the chain with a sure and certain grasp.
You cut him twice and made him bleed but Willard didn't care;
Around your neck he hung the locket and with love he placed it there.

Willard proved that his love for you could last beyond death's door,
And from now on, at Woodall Shoals his ghost will roam no more.
Your love has fought the evil and the evil has been downed —
Now Willard McVeigh is resting at the place where he was drowned.

So never take your locket off and let it never be removed,
For to your locket and to Willard's love you'll always be behooved.
So revel in the spirit of the triumph you have found,
Knowing that your joy of life is now on solid ground."

Before the women parted, they cried as they embraced,
And wondered how their lives had crossed and become so interlaced.
Their lives had flowed like rivers with independent roles
Until they flowed together at the place called Woodall Shoals.

Leah walked away from Molly's house and by the river she did stroll
And contemplated many things as she watched the river roll.
She thought about the locket and the power that it held
To resurrect a love with which an evil had been felled.

It was by a wild, demonic passion that Willard had been driven,
But by the love in Molly's locket his wicked ways were riven.
It was twilight there at Woodall where Willard's hate dissolved,
And Willard's quest for Molly's love was then and there resolved.

With her back against a river rock Leah gently fell to sleeping,
And the memories of her recent past her mind was quietly reaping.
As she slept, a dream appeared of her Bobby, and he was smiling;
His hair was blond and his eyes were blue and he was still beguiling.

"I've come to you, my Leah dear, to express my appreciation
For all you've ever done for us to enhance our love's elation.
By the river, the storm, and then the ghost, you have been assailed;
Those awful evils gave their best, but my Leah, you prevailed.

Listen to me, my Leah dear, and I'll tell you what is true:
If our lives had been reversed, I'd have done the same for you.
The love you've shown for me, my Leah, will never be forsaken,
And when you come to the end of life and after death awaken,

I'll be there and waiting for you at some celestial river bend
Where I'll kiss your lips and we'll embrace, and the river we'll descend.
There is only one, and you're that one, and my heart is yours forever,
So live your life and have your fun in whatever you endeavor.

But so you won't forget me, Leah, among life's varied themes,
I'll sometimes ride the rapids, dear, through your earthly dreams."
When Leah awoke with misty eyes, it was near the end of the day;
She dried her tears and smiled at the river as it rambled on its way.

Most memory stones have washed away through the river banks of time,
And only a few are left today to enhance the poet's rhyme.
It won't be long and I'll leave this life and I'll come this way no more;
I'll scratch my name on a river rock to brace the river lore.

My story happened long ago, but the river sings refrains
About the place where truth was lost but legend still remains.
Woodall Shoals is rolling still, and it's a dangerous place to go —
Take care; take care when you approach the wild whitewater's flow.

With Molly's talk and Bobby's dream, I was given wise directions;
I've lived my life with joy and grace without any sad reflections.
There was little left when Molly died, and even less to see;
She had no heirs and left few things, but the locket she left to me.

Around my neck at Molly's request the golden locket swings,
A symbol of the river ride to which my memory clings.
Some say that Willard lingers on at Woodall at twilight,
And lots of things are said and thought at campfires burning bright.

Tales are told where children lie in double poster beds,
And children fear the things they fear with covers on their heads.
The river has taken the rock of truth and worn it every day
To expose new things that over the years the river has washed away.

If you look, you'll often find what often is revealed
In the places error hides to keep the truth concealed.
From time to time in many ways my story has been changed;
It's told one way and told another and is often rearranged.

A myth, a hoax, an illusion strange are what are sometimes claimed,
But like as not when critics speak it's lying that is blamed.
To those who think my story false or give it errant sway
I sometimes talk about it, and this is what I say:

The tale I've told, I've told to all with just and truthful relish,

A strange, romantic, fearsome tale no legend can embellish.

I've told the story as I know it, and I need no more relate,

And as far as I'm concerned, there is no more debate.

It was a demon's deliverance by a locket engraved

That freed up the river where the demon had raved.

There is no doubt that I owe my life to that locket of Molly Cole's

And there is no doubt that I was saved from the Ghost of Woodall Shoals.

The End

This is a folk song unrelated to the poem, but which also refers to
the death of Willard McVeigh, as sung to the tune of "Down in the
Valley"

The Ballad of Woodall Shoals

Down by the river, where the misery was sown
Late in the evening hear the ghost moan
Hear the ghost moan, dear, hear the ghost moan
Late in the evening, hear the ghost moan

Down in the river, lie Willard's old bones
They're lying at Woodall, and they're covered with stones
Covered with stones, dear, they're covered with stones
Down in the river they're covered with stones

Willard loved Molly as violets love dew
Though Willard had cheated, his love was still true
She wouldn't forgive him, and their marriage was through
Their marriage was through, dear, their marriage was through

When Willard lost Molly, he wanted to die
His big heart was broken and his life went awry
His life went awry, dear, his life went awry
His big heart was broken and his life went awry

He drowned in the river he drowned at the shoals
He lies there at Woodall where the cold water rolls
Where the cold water rolls, dear, where the cold water rolls
He lies there at Woodall where the cold water rolls

Hear the shoals moan, dear, hear the shoals moan
He's calling to Molly to try to atone
To try to atone, dear, to try to atone
He's calling to Molly to try to atone

Willard keeps calling, calling her please
Calling for Molly to give his heart ease
Give his heart ease, dear, give his heart ease
Calling for Molly to give his heart ease

Down by the river, down where it rolls
Down by the river, down by the shoals
Willard loves Molly, down where it rolls
Willard loves Molly, down by the shoals

For more information on the poem, the song and the tragedy on
the Chattooga River, please visit http://ghost.trilogus.com.

Made in the USA
Middletown, DE
11 May 2022